The Life of Plants

Plant Growth

Richard & Louise Spilsbury

Heinemann
LIBRARY

Chicago, Illinois

Customer Service 888-454-2279
Visit our website at www.heinemannraintree.com

Design: Victoria Bevan and Planman Technologies
Illustrations: Jeff Edwards
Printed and bound in China by CTPS

12 11 10 09 08
10 9 8 7 6 5 4 3 2 1

**Library of Congress Cataloging-in-Publication
Data**
Spilsbury, Louise.
Plant growth / Louise and Richard Spilsbury
    v. cm. -- (Life of Plants)
Includes bibliographical references (p.).
Contents: What is growth?--How growth works-
-Germination--Roots and shoots--Getting water-
-Getting nutrients--Getting light--Leaves--Making
food--Using food--Insect-eating plants--Letting
others do the work--Staying healthy--Helping plants
grow--Ways of growing--Growth forms--Growth
cycles--When a plant dies--Try it yourself.
ISBN 978-1-4329-1500-1 (hbk)
ISBN 978-1-4329-1507-0 (pbk)
1. Growth (Plants)--Juvenile literature. 2. Plants--
Development--Juvenile literature. [1. Growth
(Plants). 2. Plants. 3. Plant life cycles.] I. Spilsbury,
Richard, 1963- II. Title. III Series.
   QK731 .S765 2002
   571.8'2--dc21
                          2001008300

Acknowledgments
The publishers would like to thank the following
for permission to reproduce photographs:
© FLPA p. **24** (Frans Lanting); © Getty Images/
Dorling Kindersley p. **35** (Peter Anderson);
© Getty Images/Stone p. **17** (Cathlyn Melloan);
© Holt Studios pp. **5**, **6**, **7**, **8**, **9**, **10**, **11**, **12**, **15**,
16, **19**, **20**, **23**, **25**, **29**, **30**, **33**, **34**, **36**, **37**, **39**;
© NHPA p. **22**; © Oxford Scientific Films pp. **4**,
13, **14**, **18**, **21**, **26**, **27**, **28**, **31**, **38**; © Science
Photo Library/Biology Media p. **32**; leaf motif:
© Photodisc.

Cover photograph of a bracken shoot reproduced
with permission of NHPA/Stephen Dalton.

The publishers would like to thank Andrew
Solway and Ann Fullick for their assistance in the
preparation of this book.

Every effort has been made to contact copyright
holders of any material reproduced in this book.
Any omissions will be rectified in subsequent
printings if notice is given to the publishers.

Disclaimer
All the Internet addresses (URLs) given in this
book were valid at the time of going to press.
However, due to the dynamic nature of the
Internet, some addresses may have changed,
or sites may have changed or ceased to exist since
publication. While the author and publishers
regret any inconvenience this may cause readers,
no responsibility for any such changes can be
accepted by either the author or the publishers.

Contents

Any words appearing in the text in bold, **like this**, are explained in the glossary.

A plant may be called different things in different countries, so every type of plant has a Latin name that can be recognized anywhere in the world. Latin names are made of two words: the first is the genus (general group) a plant belongs to and the second is its species (specific) name. Latin plant names are given in parentheses throughout this book.

What Is Growth?

As you stand beneath the arching branches of a mighty tree, it is hard to imagine that it began life as a tiny **seed**, perhaps hundreds of years ago. All living things—plants and animals—grow and become bigger. Growth is a very important part of life.

When a plant begins its life, it is small and weak. One of the reasons it grows is to become stronger and bigger. This makes it better able to obtain the things it needs to live and to survive any challenges that might come its way, ranging from a fierce storm to a hungry **grazing animal**. The other reason that living things grow is to reach adulthood and be able to produce young like themselves, which will live on after they have died.

The trees that time forgot!

Did you know that the oldest living things on Earth are trees? In California there is a bristlecone pine (*Pinus longaeva*), similar to the one in the photo, that is 4,765 years old. It is amazing to think that Methuselah, as the tree is called, was a sapling (young tree) when the ancient Egyptians were busy building their pyramids!

How quickly do plants grow?

Humans grow fastest as babies and very young children. After that we grow more slowly, except perhaps for a growth spurt when we are teenagers. When we reach adulthood, we stop growing. We get older and we may gain or lose weight, but we do not grow any taller and our feet do not grow any longer. Plants, on the other hand, continue growing throughout their entire lives. Even when they have grown to maturity, many plants still continue growing.

While most people grow at roughly the same rate, different plants grow at very different rates. Some plants grow quickly and others grow more slowly. A type of bamboo plant from Myanmar (Burma) has thick **stems** that can increase in height by up to 18 inches (46 centimeters) a day! The record for being the slowest-growing plant goes to a Mexican palm-like plant called *Dioon edule*. These plants may live for up to 3,000 years, but often grow less than 0.4 inches (1 centimeter) taller each year!

Bamboo plants like these in Columbia are one of the fastest-growing **species** of plants in the world.

How Growth Works

All living things are made up of millions of tiny living parts called **cells**. Cells are the basic units of life, and different types of cells form the different parts of all **organisms** (living things). The size of a living thing is not related to the size of its cells. (Cells are so incredibly tiny that they can usually only be seen through a microscope.) Rather, size is related to the number of cells that a living thing contains.

Making more cells

In order to grow, living things need to increase the number of cells in their body. Most plants start life as a **seed**, made up of a certain number of cells. To grow into a new plant and increase in size, each cell in the seed divides in two in order to

create two cells. Then those two divide again, making four cells. The cells continue dividing like this, and as they increase in number, different groups of cells begin to specialize, developing into specific types of cells. These different types of cells form the different parts of the plant. Some types of cells form the leaves. Others become the petals of a flower or the **roots** that grow under the ground.

An oak tree is much bigger than a primrose because it has trillions more cells in each of the parts that make up its giant body.

What plants need to grow

The cells that make up every living thing need **energy** to live and increase their number. Humans and other animals get the energy they need from food, which they find, hunt, or buy. Plants also need food to provide them with energy for growth, but they cannot move around to get it. Plants are able to make their own food, using a process called **photosynthesis**. The things they need to carry out this process are water, light, and air.

To grow well, plants also need **nutrients**, space, and the right temperature. But different plants require different amounts of all these things—too much or too little of any one may slow down or even stop a plant's growth. In this book we are going to find out how a plant uses its parts to get the right amounts of what it needs to make it grow, and what else it needs to make its growth successful.

Successful growth

Plants are the largest living things on Earth. Giant redwood trees (*Sequoiadendron giganteum*) can grow up to 2,750 tons in weight. Blue whales are the largest creatures in the animal kingdom, and even the biggest blue whale cannot compete with a giant redwood, weighing in at a mere 220 tons.

Starting to Grow

Most plants start life as a **seed**. Seeds have a tough outer coat that protects the contents. Inside the seed there is an **embryo** (a tiny baby plant), which consists of a tiny **root** and a **shoot**. A seed is a bit like an egg with a baby chicken growing inside. Just like an egg, the seed contains a food store. This store of food keeps the embryo alive and fuels the start of growth in the seed, which is known as **germination**.

When the time is right

A plant makes seeds in its flowers. When the seeds are fully grown, the parent plant releases the seeds. Some of these seeds are eaten by animals and some land in places that are unsuitable for plant growth, but a few land in the right type of soil for the plant to grow. Some seeds germinate right away, but many do not germinate for weeks, months, or even years. The seed is able to survive until the conditions are just right. Most seeds need three things before they are able to germinate: water, air, and warmth. In countries where a cold winter is followed by a warm spring, many seeds will not start to grow until the days begin to get warmer and there are more hours of daylight. These are the signals the seed needs to start to germinate.

seed coat

Most seeds are able to wait a long time until the conditions for germination are just right. This runner bean seed has a tough outer coat, which protects the young plant inside.

Germination begins

While the seed lies in the soil, waiting for the right conditions for germination, it dries out a little. When germination begins, the seed soaks up lots of water from the soil around it. Inside the seed, the young root and shoot start to grow. As they grow, they become too big for the seed and crack the seed's hard shell. The first sign of life is the young root. It forces its way out of one end of the seed and starts to grow down into the soil. The shoot is the next part of the plant to emerge. The young shoot with the plant's first **stem** and leaves pushes its way up, out of the top of the seed.

A long wait

In some of the world's hottest deserts, rain may fall only once every few years. Seeds may have to wait a very long time until there is enough water for them to germinate. Seeds survive the dry periods underneath the ground. When the rains come, buried seeds suddenly burst into flower. It is as if someone has waved a magic wand. The empty desert is transformed into a sea of color like this one in Antelope Valley, California. This magnificent spectacle lasts only a few days or weeks. Then the harsh sun dries up the flowers and the plants die, leaving only the sand once more.

Roots and Shoots

The **root** is the first part of the plant to start growing. After it has emerged from the broken **seed** case, it grows straight down into the soil. Roots almost always grow downward because they respond to the pull of **gravity**, the force that makes things fall to the ground when we drop them. Even if a seed lands in the soil the wrong way up or there is a stone in the way, the root will wind around until it can grow downward.

Different plants grow different types of roots. In some plants, such as carrots, there is one main root, which becomes quite thick and long. Smaller, thinner roots grow from this main root, branching out to the sides. Other plants, such as leeks, may have many roots of roughly the same size. All roots are strong, however small they may be. As roots burrow deeper into the soil, they bump into stones and other obstacles, such as other roots. Outer layers of the cap (tip) of the root rub off to help the root move more smoothly through the soil.

One of the jobs that roots do is to anchor the plant in the soil. Roots give the plant a firm grip on the ground so the shoot can start growing up.

Going up—shoots

After the root has started to grow, the shoot begins to break out of the seed case. **Shoots** grow in the opposite direction from roots: they always grow upward, toward the light. The tip of the shoot is able to detect light, so the plant knows which direction to grow.

The shoot pushes its way up until it emerges above the soil. If you look carefully at the shoots of very young plants, you may be able to see the seed cases still attached to the top of the shoot. Once the shoot is in the light, it straightens up and the first leaves are revealed. As the leaves grow, the seed case falls off and drops to the ground. There, having completed its task, it rots away.

When germination is complete

The early growth of the roots and shoot is fueled by the food stored in the seed. In some seeds the food store is kept in the tiny leaves on the shoot. These are known as seed leaves. In others, it is stored around the **embryo**. Once the plant has established a root system and has grown its first true leaves (leaves that look like the leaves on the parent plant), **germination** is properly complete. The young plant now has all the things that it needs to make food for itself.

The narrow leaves at the bottom of this corn poppy are its seed leaves. They provide food for the seed to germinate. Once the plant's true leaves, nearer the top, have formed, the seed leaves die. They are no longer needed.

Getting Water

Water is essential for all living things. Believe it or not, you (and other animals) are mainly made up of water, which is in the **cells** that make up your body. Water accounts for around 95 percent of the weight of a plant, and many smaller plants rely on the water inside them to hold them upright. Plants not only depend on water to form their parts, they also need water to be able to make their own food in the process of **photosynthesis**.

Plants take in water through their **roots**. Plants that grow in ponds or lakes have a continuous supply of water all around them. Plants that grow on the land take in water from the soil. If the soil where a plant grows is very dry, its roots may have to grow very deep in order to find enough moisture. In woodland that is full of trees with deep roots, other plants may grow roots just below the surface of the soil. That way they can gather rainwater as it falls, before it soaks away into deeper ground.

Smaller plants can survive among the roots of bigger trees because they have shallow root systems that can soak up rainwater before it drains down to the large tree roots below.

Root hairs

Water is sucked into a plant by the tiny root hairs that grow at the ends of its smaller roots. Root hairs on many plants are so small and thin that it is tricky to see them without using a magnifying glass. It is the fact that root hairs are so little that makes them so good at their job. They can grow around the fragments of stones and soil to find the water that is trapped between them. Also, there are so many root hairs that they greatly increase the plant's ability to take in water from the soil. After the root hairs collect the water, it is passed on to the smaller roots. From these the water travels into the main roots and finally up into the **stem** of the plant or trunk of a tree, and then into its leaves.

Taking a cutting

To grow a new plant from an old one, first, cut off a small piece of the stem. Then, dip the stem into some **hormone rooting powder**. The powder contains the special chemicals (**hormones**) that make roots grow. When the stem cells are dipped in the powder, they form roots. With roots, the cutting can take up water and **minerals** from soil to supply its own **shoots** and leaves. You have your new plant!

The root on this radish seedling (young plant) is covered in white root hairs. Each hair helps the plant take in more water from the soil.

Getting Nutrients

Although plants can make their own food by **photosynthesis**, they also need other substances to help them grow and thrive. We call these substances **nutrients**, because they nourish the plant. Most plants take in nutrients from soil.

What is soil?

Soil is a mixture of tiny pieces of rock and the remains of decayed plants and animals. It is formed when rocks are gradually broken up by wind and rain. As decayed leaves and dead plants and animals rot away, they are washed into the ground and also become part of the soil. So, soil contains nutrients from decayed living things and **minerals** from rock fragments.

Nutrients in water

Many of these nutrients and minerals are **dissolved** in water that is found in soil. Plants take in these nutrients and minerals when they take in water through their **roots**. Water travels up from the roots through the rest of the plant in a set of tubes called **xylem**. Xylem in a plant are like the pipes in a house, transporting water from one part to another.

This magnified picture of the inside of a root shows the xylem tubes that run through the whole plant.

Transpiration

The way plants take in water is a little like the way you drink with a straw. As water leaves the top of a straw (when it is sucked into your mouth), more water fills the space left at the bottom of the straw. In plants, water travels through xylem tubes in the leaves. As water is lost from these tubes at the top of the plant, more water comes into the bottom of the tubes (in the roots) to replace it. The process is called **transpiration**.

Water escapes from the leaves because it **evaporates** and passes out of little holes on a leaf's surface, called **stomata**. As the sun warms the leaves, the water inside them heats up, too. This makes some of the water evaporate, which means it turns into an invisible gas called **water vapor** and passes out of the stomata into the air. It is a bit like the way a T-shirt dries on a clothes line. As the air warms the fabric, water within it evaporates, leaving your T-shirt dry.

Thirsty trees!

On a warm day, a tree takes in about 250 gallons (1,130 liters) of water. That is enough to fill five bathtubs! It takes in this much to replace water that it loses through its many leaves.

As water vapor released from rain forest trees cools, it changes back into droplets of water, forming dense clouds.

Getting Light

If you move a houseplant from a sunny windowsill to a dark cupboard, it will soon become pale and weak, and eventually it will die. Plants cannot survive without some light—they need it to live and to grow. Plants collect light through their leaves, and they have different ways of making sure their leaves are in the best positions to receive light.

For some plants it is a question of timing. Flowering plants that live on a woodland floor grow new leaves early in the spring. That way they get the light they need to produce flowers before the trees fill out with leaves and block the precious rays. Trees have tall **stems**, called trunks, supporting their branches. Their leaves grow from twigs on branches, which spread out like arms to hold the leaves out into the daylight. Branches in the **canopy** (upper part) of a tree grow so that their leaves do not overlap and block light from others.

Some plants use other ways to hold their leaves up to the light. Bladderwrack (*Fucus vesiculosis*) is a type of seaweed. It has balloons of air within its leaves that make the leaves float near the water's surface, where there is the most light.

The branches on this tree grow so that their leaves do not stop the light from reaching other leaves. This makes the canopy look like a giant green jigsaw puzzle.

Light and shade

Most leaves need a certain amount of light. If there is not enough, a leaf will not be able to make enough food to survive. If there is too much light, it can damage the parts within the leaf that make the plant's food.

All leaves have an outer layer called a **cuticle**. The cuticle is usually **waxy**, and it helps to protect the fragile inner parts of the leaf. On leaves of plants such as ferns, which live in shade, it is thinner. This allows the leaves to absorb (take in) as much light as they can. Plants growing in bright sunlight have a thicker cuticle. Some sunlight still gets through, but the cuticle protects the leaf from the strongest rays. In hot places, some leaves also have little hairs growing on them. These help to filter (break up) the sunlight's harsh rays.

Growing toward the light

Light is essential for plants to make their own food. If light comes from one direction, plant **shoots** respond by growing toward it. **Roots**, however, respond by growing away from light. These growth responses are called **tropisms**. Plant **cells** grow in response to chemicals called plant **hormones**. If light hits a shoot on one side, the hormone moves to the shaded side. As a result of the extra hormone, the cells on the shady side of the shoot grow faster, and the shoot bends over toward the light.

Leaves

Leaves are often called the plant's food factory. This is because food is made inside the leaves by a process called **photosynthesis**. Just like any other factory, work cannot begin until all the raw materials are in place. The raw materials that a leaf factory needs to make food are water and **carbon dioxide** (a gas in the air).

Water deliveries

Plants take in water through their **roots**, so how do they transport it all the way up to their leaves? The answer is that within the roots, **stems**, and leaves of a plant there is a network of water-carrying tubes called **xylem**. The water moves from the roots to the stem and on into the leaves through these xylem tubes.

What is a vascular plant?

Plants that have tubes in their roots, leaves, and stems to transport water are called **vascular plants**. Vascular means "having vessels." A vessel is a tube or pipe that carries a fluid. Most of the plants in the world are vascular. Some plants, such as **mosses,** are different. All the parts of these plants can absorb water and **nutrients**, so they do not need tubes to transport them.

This is a leaf skeleton. The softer green part has rotted away, leaving only the tougher veins of the leaf. These veins are tiny tubes, some of which are used to transport water all through the leaves.

Collecting carbon dioxide

Plants take carbon dioxide straight from the air into their leaves through tiny openings called **stomata**. Leaves have hundreds of stomata, but they are so tiny that you cannot usually see them. In some plants, most of the stomata are on the underside of the leaf. In others, there are stomata both on the top and on the underside of the leaf.

The stomata are also the holes through which **water vapor** escapes in **transpiration**. They can open and close to stop the leaf from losing more water. Each hole is flanked by two guard **cells**, which open the stomata when they bend outward and close it when they bend inward. Most plants open their stomata during daylight hours, when photosynthesis usually occurs, and close them at night.

Talking to plants

Do you know that some people believe talking to plants helps them grow? This may not be as crazy as it sounds. When you breathe out, you release carbon dioxide from your body into the air. When you speak to a plant, you breathe this carbon dioxide toward its leaves. Since plants need this gas to make food, perhaps talking to them isn't such a bad idea after all!

This magnified picture of part of a leaf shows its stomata. You can see the two curved guard cells, which open and close the stomata, on either side of the holes.

Making Food

Once the raw materials—the **carbon dioxide** and water—are in place, the leaf factory is ready to start work on food production. There is just one thing missing: like all factories, the leaf needs a source of power. While an ordinary factory uses gas or electricity, the power source for **photosynthesis** is sunlight, which the plant absorbs through its leaves.

Light trap

Daylight is essential to the process of photosynthesis. In fact the word "photosynthesis" means "putting together with light." The leaf traps light using a remarkable **pigment** called **chlorophyll**. Chlorophyll is green, and it is what gives leaves their green color. You may have noticed that leaves are usually a darker green on the top side than on the underside. That is because there is more chlorophyll on the top of the leaf, where most of the sunlight falls. Even leaves that do not look green, such as the red leaves of a copper beech tree (*Fagus cuprea*), contain chlorophyll. You just cannot see it because in certain plants other colors hide the green.

Photosynthesis occurs near the top surface of a leaf, where the sunlight is at its strongest. That is why most of the leaf's chlorophyll is concentrated in the top surface, making the upper part of a leaf look far greener than the bottom.

Chlorophyll is made in tiny compartments called **chloroplasts** within each leaf **cell**. The food-making cells within the leaves are packed with these chloroplasts. Chloroplasts use their chlorophyll to absorb sunlight. Then they use the sunlight's **energy** to combine the carbon dioxide and water to make food in the form of sugars.

Gas works

Inside droplets of water there are two different kinds of gas: hydrogen and **oxygen**. The leaf splits the water into these separate parts. Then, the hydrogen is combined with the carbon dioxide to form sugars. The plant uses some of the oxygen that is left and releases the rest into the air through the **stomata** (tiny openings) on its leaves. Now the plant can use the sugars—its "food"—to fuel its own growth.

Photosynthesis and us

Photosynthesis is one of the most important things in the world. Without it not only would plants die, but we would, too! During photosynthesis, plants release oxygen through their stomata. This oxygen is a very important part of the air that we breathe. This means that plants are essential to our survival in two ways. First, they are the source of all our food, whether we eat the plants themselves or animals that eat plants. Second, if all the plants in the world died out, humans and animals would soon die from lack of oxygen.

The little green circles you can see in this picture of Canadian pond weed cells are chloroplasts. The cells have been magnified about 200 times.

Using Food

The food or sugars made by the plant in **photosynthesis** move out of the leaf in tubes called **phloem**. The phloem tubes contain water, which mixes with the sugars to form a sweet liquid called **sap**. The sap flows along the phloem tubes from the leaf, through the **stem**, and on to all the other parts of the plant.

Storing food

The plant uses some of the sugars right away, to provide the **energy** it needs to grow, and it stores the rest. Most plants change extra sugars into starches, another type of food. Starch is easier for the plant to store than sugar. Some starches are stored in underground plant parts, such as a **root** or an underground stem. (Potatoes and carrots are underground food stores. The reason we eat vegetables like carrots and potatoes is that we can also use the stored food for ourselves.) The plant can turn the starch back into sugar when it needs more energy—for example, when it is time to grow flowers and make **seeds**.

The syrup tree

The maple syrup you pour over a pancake is actually the sap of the sugar maple tree (*Acer saccharum*). Farmers drill holes into the wood until they reach the phloem and collect some of the sap that flows out. The sap is clear and slightly sweet and has to be boiled down to make the thick, sweet syrup that we buy.

Turning food into energy

A car engine gets the energy it needs to move from fuel. Plants and animals get the energy they need to live and grow from food. When an engine uses gasoline, it has to burn it with **oxygen** to produce energy. When plants and animals make energy from their food, they use oxygen in a similar way.

Respiration

The process by which living things use oxygen to release energy from their food is called **respiration**. Some people think that respiration means breathing. In fact, breathing is just what animals do to get oxygen into their bodies and **carbon dioxide** out. Plants have three ways of obtaining the oxygen they need. They create an oxygen supply for themselves during photosynthesis, they take in oxygen through the **stomata** in their leaves, and they absorb oxygen through their roots (during **transpiration**) from tiny pockets of air in the soil.

In respiration, plants mix the oxygen with sugars within their **cells**. This special mixing releases energy. The cells can then use this energy to divide and increase their number in order for the plants to grow, and also to repair themselves when damaged. Along with energy, respiration also produces carbon dioxide, a gas that plants can use in photosynthesis.

When it is time to grow flowers and produce seeds, plants convert some of the food made in photosynthesis to fuel the new growth.

Feeding on Others

One group of plants does not use **photosynthesis** to make food. These plants are the burglars of the plant world because they survive by stealing food from other plants. They are called **parasites**, and the plants that they feed off are known as "hosts"—even though the plants that feed on them are anything but welcome guests.

Many parasitic plants live in the shade because they do not need the sunlight for photosynthesis. Many do not have green leaves for the same reason. Some do not even have **roots** in the ground like other plants. They use their roots to attach themselves to other plants and to penetrate their stems and take the food that flows through the tubes—the **xylem** and **phloem**—inside. Other parasitic plants have roots in the soil, and they attach themselves to host plants by suckers, which grow out of their stem and into the other plant's stem. Some parasitic plants take so much food from the host plant that they starve it. Others seem to be able to take all the **nutrients** they need without destroying their host.

The giant rafflesia (*Rafflesia arnoldii*) is one of the most impressive parasites in the world. A single flower can weigh up to 15 pounds (7 kilograms) and grow up to 3 feet (1 meter) wide.

Dodder

The dodder (*Cuscuta*) is a good example of a parasite that attaches itself to a host plant using its stems. Dodder plants have string-like **tendrils** (long, very thin leaves) that stretch across the ground. If they reach a plant that is too thin or weak, they ignore it. When they reach a healthy plant, they wrap themselves around its stem and grip on tightly with suckers. The suckers pierce the stem and find their way into the host's food vessels. Using food from its host, the dodder is then able to grow very quickly until it almost covers the host plant. Then it continues on in search of another victim.

Mistletoe

Mistletoe plants (*Viscum album*) attach themselves to other plants using their roots. Adult mistletoe plants produce white berries that birds feed on. These are so sticky that to get rid of the **seed** after eating the fruit, the bird rubs its beak onto branches or cracks in tree bark. Thus settled, the seed grows a root that forces itself into the cracks of the branch and into the tubes that carry the tree's **sap**. It then sucks up this food for its own use.

Mistletoe plants feed off a tree's food supply, but they have green leaves, so they also make some of their food by photosynthesis. Plants like this are known as partial parasites.

Insect-Eating Plants

Most plants in the world have to cope with being eaten by insects, which are greedy for the food that is stored in their leaves or **roots** or is carried in their **stems**. Some plants, however, eat insects instead!

Although they make their own food by **photosynthesis**, most insect-eating plants live in sandy, rocky, or boggy soils that are not very rich in **nutrients**. Plants catch insects to get the extra nutrients they need for healthy growth. Usually they trap the insects in some way and then use special juices to **dissolve** them. The juices break the insects down into smaller and smaller pieces until they become liquid. This liquid then passes easily into the plant.

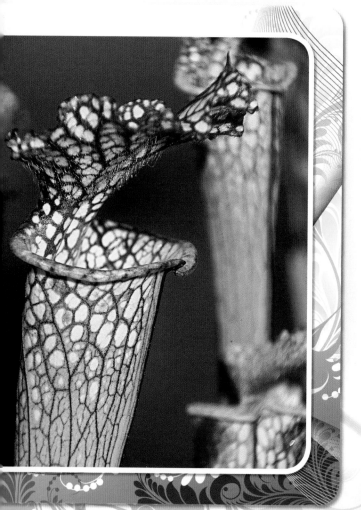

Pitcher plants (*Nepenthes*) are some of the best-known insect-eaters. There are many different kinds, but they all attract insects with sweet-smelling **nectar**. Pitcher plants have special tube-shaped leaves, which look like green jugs or "pitchers." When the insects enter the pitcher, they lose their grip and fall to the bottom. The sides of the pitcher are slippery, so it is impossible for them to crawl out. They splash down into a pool of liquid at the bottom of the pitcher and quickly drown. The insect gradually dissolves and is absorbed into the plant's system.

This North American pitcher plant (*Sarracenia leucophylla*) has a type of lid above the top of the pitcher to stop rain from getting in.

Sundews

Round-leafed sundews (*Drosera rotundifolia*) live in **peat bogs**. They supplement (add to) their diet by catching insects, trapping them on sticky hairs that are on their long, curly leaves. At the end of each hair is a drop of sticky liquid. The liquid has a smell that attracts insects. When an insect lands on one of the hairs, it gets stuck in the liquid. Its struggles cause neighboring hairs to curl around the insect. These hairs hold the insect tight while the plant's juices dissolve the insect. The plant then absorbs the juices and makes use of the nutrients they provide.

A plant that can count?

At the end of the narrow green leaves of the Venus flytrap (*Dionaea muscipula*) are two flat, rounded lobes. These offer insects a landing pad to rest on while they drink nectar there. This spot is advertised by a patch of red. In fact the lobes form a deadly trap. To stop the trap from springing shut for no good reason—for example, when a raindrop falls on it—the plant counts! Each lobe has a few hairs. If a fly touches only one of these hairs, the trap stays open. If it touches two or more, the trap snaps shut and the spikes on the edges of the leaves interlock to form a cage. The teeth of these green jaws stay closed as the plant juices digest the fly.

Staying Healthy

Plants need healthy parts to be able to grow well, but they often find themselves under attack. Insects use their sucking mouthparts to puncture the **stems** of plants to get at the sugary **sap** that flows within. Animals such as rabbits and deer eat plants' leaves and **roots**. In order to protect themselves against the insects and animals that regularly try to feed on them, some plants have defense systems.

Plant defenses

Plants use spikes, thorns, stings, poison, and even water traps to scare off their enemies. Some plants are able to avoid tiny insects with a set of fine hairs across their leaves. This makes it difficult for smaller insects to land or walk on the

leaves. The thorns on the stem of a rose (*Rosa*) can be very painful for **grazing animals**, so the animals soon learn to leave it alone. Some holly (*Ilex*) leaves are edged with curled prickles, which soon scare off any would-be diners.

On a teasel plant (*Dipsacus*) the leaves grow in pairs, and where they meet at the stem a cup-shaped pool forms. This fills with rainwater. When insects and small snails climb onto the leaves to eat them, many slide into this pool and drown!

Bracken's lethal weapon

Bracken (*Pteridium aquilinum*) covers hillsides in almost every continent of the world except Antarctica. One of the reasons a bracken plant is so successful is that it protects itself with deadly poisons that are released only when its leaves are chewed by animals. Large bracken plants make enough of these poisons to cause blindness or even cancer in grazing animals, such as rabbits and deer. Animals soon learn to steer clear of bracken, leaving the plant free to grow and spread far and wide.

How do stinging nettles sting?

Have you ever been stung by a stinging nettle (*Urtica dioica*)? It hurts so much that most of us do our best to avoid them if we can. Imagine how that sting feels to a smaller animal, such as a rabbit, and how efficiently it must make them want to avoid trying to eat the nettle's lush green leaves. How does it work? Stinging nettle leaves and stems are covered with tiny hairs that have sharp, pointed ends. The tip of these hairs can be broken off by even the gentlest touch. The broken edges are so sharp that they cut the skin of whatever animal touches the plant. At the same time, a poison stored in the base of the hair is released and squirted into the wound.

Helping Plants Grow

When gardeners or farmers grow plants for pleasure or to sell, they use their knowledge of what plants need to help them produce bigger and better plants. They can also grow plants from other countries and climates by giving them what they need artificially.

All plants need water, but farmers can grow plants in very dry soils by pumping water into the ground. This is called **irrigation**. Farmers also add **fertilizers** to soil. Fertilizers are **nutrients** that help to increase the amount and quality of the crops. People sometimes put "plant food" onto houseplants. This is also a type of fertilizer. As they grow, houseplants use up all the nutrients that are in the pot's soil, so people add plant food to replace the nutrients.

Gardeners and farmers often use greenhouses and plastic tunnels to provide plants with artificial warmth and shelter. The extra warmth helps the seeds to **germinate**. The plants grow better than they would if they had been planted directly outside. Some plants are kept in artificial conditions all the time. Hothouses, like those in botanical gardens, have heaters so that people can grow heat-loving exotic plants such as tropical flowers.

Plant producers can control the time plants flower so they are ready exactly when consumers want them. These poinsettias (*Euphorbia pulcherrima*) are ready for Christmas.

Hydroponics

Hydroponics is a way of growing plants without soil. Instead, scientists grow plants in containers of water or small stones, such as coarse sand or gravel. They ensure the plants get everything they would normally get from soil: water, air, and nutrients. Plants grown in water do not have anything for their **roots** to hold on to, so they grow through a wire mesh, which holds them up. Their roots hang down, taking in water that has nutrients added to it. Plants growing in soil also take in **oxygen** from the ground. So, without soil, oxygen needs to be pumped into the water for the plant to use. Plants grown in containers of coarse sand or gravel can use their roots to anchor themselves, so they do not need any support. The grains of sand or gravel have air between them, but no nutrients or water. Water that contains nutrients is pumped up from below or sprinkled on these containers from above.

Growing plants by hydroponics does not make the plants bigger or better, but it is a useful way of finding out what plants need to grow well. Scientists can change the amounts or types of nutrients they give particular plants to see what produces the most successful growth.

Hydroponics is a good way to learn what plants need. It also proves that they do not necessarily need soil to grow!

Ways of Growing

In many plants, growth is concentrated at certain points. Most growth occurs at the very top or bottom of a plant, such as the tips of leaves, twigs, or **roots**. When leaves and **stems** grow longer and roots reach deeper into the soil, most of the plant's growth happens just behind the tips or ends of the plant parts. For example, in a root the main growing point is at the tip of the root. There, **cells** divide and increase in number to make the root increase in length. Other plants, such as grasses, grow from their base.

Weedkillers—stopping growth

A weed is a plant growing where it is not wanted. Some weedkillers use plant **hormones** to kill the plants. The plant takes in the hormone through the roots or the leaves. The hormone makes the cells in the **meristems** divide very quickly. The plants grow too fast. They use up their food stores. Soon the weeds "outgrow" themselves and die. Hormone weedkillers are poisonous to plants, but quite safe for animals and humans.

Under the microscope

Cell division

Cell division in plants usually takes place in special areas, called meristems, just behind the tip of the stem or root. In the meristems the cells divide, get longer and bigger, and then turn into all the different types of cells needed to make a plant. This **micrograph** shows cells dividing in an onion.

Tree growth

Trees grow in two different ways at the same time. As with other plants, they grow taller and deeper by growing at the tips of their twigs and roots. The trunk grows taller from the top and the roots grow longer. This means that when a branch grows out sideways from a trunk, it will always be the same height above the ground.

Trees, trunks, branches, twigs, and roots can also grow wider. All of these parts are covered in bark. Just below the bark is an area of growth called the **cambium**. When cells there divide, the parts of the tree get wider. It is important for trees to grow wide trunks because they need to be very strong to support their many heavy branches.

World's widest tree

The widest tree ever known grew in Sicily, Italy, and reached its greatest size in the late 18th century. This European chestnut tree (*Castanea sativa*) was given the grand nickname "Tree of 100 horses" because it measured a mighty 190 feet (57.9 meters) in circumference. It is still alive today, but it has split into three parts.

If you look at a section of trunk, you can see lots of **annual rings**. These are formed when the cambium grows outward each year. By counting the annual rings you can find out the age of a tree.

Growth Shapes

Each **species** (type) of plant in the world grows in a typical shape. Although one sunflower is slightly different from another, they all have a tall **stem** with a large yellow flower head at the top. While one Norway spruce (*Picea abies*) may be taller and have more branches than another, they all have the same characteristic triangular shape.

Tree forms

The shape of each plant species is suited to the type of **habitat** the plant usually lives in. For example, there is a reason why Norway spruces are triangular. They usually grow in cold places and are often covered in snow in winter. Their shape, with branches angled toward the ground, means much of the snow slides off their needles. Now think of a **deciduous** tree such as a beech (*Fagus*) or maple (*Acer*). As it loses its leaves in winter, it does not have to protect them from snow. However, it usually lives in woodland where there are lots of other trees. So, it has long branches that grow up and out to make sure its leaves get enough light for **photosynthesis** to occur.

If the branches of this spruce tree spread out instead of down, the weight of heavy winter snow could seriously damage them.

Responding to the environment

Although all plant species try to grow in their characteristic shape, an individual plant grows to a shape that is affected by the environment in which it lives.

The amount of light, **nutrients**, water, space, and heat a plant gets all affect how it grows. A bean plant grown in a shady spot is likely to be much paler and weaker than one grown in sunlight. If a **seed germinates** in soil without the right nutrients, the young plant may become unhealthy and develop blotchy leaves or weak stems. An ivy plant (*Hedera helix*) will grow to the shape and height of the wall it is using to support itself. On some windswept coastal paths, trees such as blackthorn (*Prunus spinosa*), which would normally grow upright, grow hunched and stunted. Usually they do not blow over. Instead, they grow less on the side facing the wind, so that they bend away from the wind.

Light and shade

Plants need to fit in with their habitats. If a plant grows in bright sunlight, it does not need to waste **energy** growing large leaves because it can make enough food with smaller ones. A similar plant growing in a shady spot will have much bigger leaves. It must trap enough sunlight to make the food it needs, so it has to produce a large leaf area.

Growth Cycles

The human growth cycle usually goes like this: we are born, we grow from children to adults (when we may have children of our own), then we grow old, and finally we die. The growth cycle is similar for plants: they grow, make flowers and **seeds**, and then die.

Annual plants take less than one year to grow from seed, to flower, to spread seeds that can survive until the next growing season, and then to die. Annual plants include flowering plants such as sunflowers (*Helianthus*) and poppies (*Papaver*).

Biennial plants take two years to complete their life cycle. In the first year they grow green leafy parts, which die back in the fall. The plants store food, usually in their **roots**, to fuel growth in the following spring. In this second year, biennial plants, such as wild carrots and foxgloves (*Digitalis*), produce their flowers and seeds, and then die.

Perennial plants, such as trees and shrubs, live for two or more years, and most produce flowers every year. Many lose their leaves or even all their parts above ground in winter or a dry season. The roots store food in order to fuel new growth the following year.

The sunflower grows, flowers, and dies in the same year, leaving its many seeds to survive and grow into new plants the next year.

Seasons

In the northern countries of the world, the growth cycles of most plants are determined by the seasons. In spring, seeds **germinate**, new plants develop, and established plants begin to grow again after resting throughout winter. In the hot summer months, plants flower and begin to produce fruits. In the fall, the fruits ripen and die, releasing the plants' seeds.

In winter, the days are shorter and there is less light for plants to use for **photosynthesis**. The freezing weather could destroy plant parts, such as leaves, so many **deciduous** trees shed their leaves and stop growing during the winter. They keep alive using food stored in their roots. When spring comes around once more, they grow new leaves and make their own food again.

Why do leaves change color?

Leaves contain many colors, but in spring and summer the green **chlorophyll** hides them. In the fall, trees stop producing new chlorophyll in the leaves and the old chlorophyll breaks down, letting other leaf colors—yellows, oranges, reds, and browns—show through. This colorful display does not last long. The trees grow a layer of **cork** across the leaf **stalks**, plugging the pipelines that carry water. The leaves dry out, die, and fall.

When a Plant Dies

The length of time an animal lives varies among different **species**. Few humans live for more than 100 years, while wolves live about 13 years, mice live 2 to 6 years, and fruit flies live less than 2 months. Different plants also have different life spans, ranging from a few months to hundreds of years. Plants, like animals, may also die before their time. **Grazing animals** may eat them or trample on them. **Parasite** plants may rob them of so much food that they starve. Sometimes humans cut plants down to clear land.

The importance of recycling

Even when a plant is dead, it still has a useful job to do. We all know how important it is to recycle as much as we can, whether it be glass bottles, newspapers, or plastics. When a plant dies, it is recycled, too. When plants and animals die, they begin to decay. Small animals and insects eat parts of them, and what is left **decomposes** (breaks down into smaller and smaller pieces) until it is washed into the soil by rainwater. The **nutrients** that were in the plants now become part of the soil. New plants use the nutrients to help them grow, and the cycle of life, death, and decay begins again.

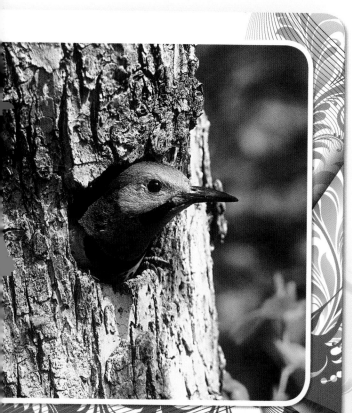

Holes in dead trees make perfect hideaways for woodland creatures, like this northern flicker (*Colaptes auratus*).

From beginning to end

We began this book with plant **germination** and have reached its conclusion with the death of a plant. To fuel the growth that takes them through life, plants make their food from the simplest ingredients imaginable. Using **energy** from the results of the incredible process of **photosynthesis**, plants can build themselves up to become complex living things. They continue growing throughout their lives, some of them developing into the largest, oldest, and heaviest living things on the planet.

The death and decay of a tree

A dead tree may take as long as 15 years to decay. A multitude of living things gradually break it down and help to release its nutrients back into the soil. Creatures such as millipedes and slugs eat dead leaves, releasing some of their nutrients into the soil when the waste passes through the animals' bodies. Gradually the bark of the tree becomes loose and pieces fall off, exposing the wood. This makes it easier for other insects and animals to eat or break into it. Once the middle of the tree is rotten, the trunk is easily broken by wind and falls to the ground. **Fungi** and **bacteria** get to work, turning the tree into a soggy pulp. Gradually all visible remains of the tree are gone.

Try It Yourself!

Try these experiments to see for yourself some of the plant processes you have learned about in this book.

Tying up trees

You will need:

- A tree
- A plastic bag
- An elastic band or string

Choose a tree at school or home that has a branch you can reach, preferably in a shady spot. Early one evening, carefully tie a small, clear plastic bag around the end of the branch, fitting in a good number of leaves. Tie the bag on tightly so that no air can escape.

Return to the tree the next morning. In your bag there should be droplets of water. These are the result of **transpiration**. Warmth has heated the water in the leaves and changed it into the gas we call **water vapor**. Usually you cannot see this, but it has cooled again and gone back to being liquid water, forming the droplets you can see in your bag!

Keep a plant in the dark

This experiment shows you what happens when plants cannot get the light that they need to make food.

You will need:

- An area of grass, either at school or at home
- A waterproof box or bowl that is opaque (you cannot see light through it)

Place your box or bowl, upside-down, over a piece of grass. Leave it there for a week. When you return, take off the box or bowl and compare the grass that was beneath it with the rest of the lawn. The grass under the box will have turned pale and floppy. Without light, it has not been able to use the process of **photosynthesis** to produce food. If you left it without light for too much longer, it would die.

Play a trick on roots

Do **roots** always grow downward? In this experiment you will try to trick a bean and see if you can change the direction in which its roots grow.

You will need:

- An old, transparent (see-through) drink bottle
- Blotting paper
- Water
- A broad bean **seed**

Carefully cut the top off the drink bottle so the top of it is flat. Take a piece of blotting paper and fold it so it will fit inside the bottle, wrapped around the inside. Wet it thoroughly before you put it inside. Slide your bean in between the paper and the bottle so that you can see it from the outside. Put the bottle somewhere warm. Check the bean after a few days. When a root begins to grow downward, turn the bottle over, so the root looks like it is growing upward. Leave the bottle for a few more days. What happens to the root?

The root should curl around so that it can continue to grow downward. If you turn the bottle a second time, the same thing should happen. Remember that roots respond to the force of **gravity**, so they will always grow down, not up.

Setting off with seeds

Growing watercress seeds is a great way to find out what seeds need to **germinate**.

You will need:

- Four small, shallow pots or trays (old margarine tubs will be fine)
- Cotton pads or cotton balls
- A packet of watercress seeds
- Water

Put a thin layer of cotton in the bottom of all four trays. Pour water on the cotton in two of the trays only. Pour any excess water away so that the cotton in these two trays is damp, not flooded. Sprinkle a thin layer of watercress seeds on all four layers of cotton.

Next, put one dry tray and one wet tray in a refrigerator. Put the other two trays somewhere warm and dark, such as a cupboard.

Check all four after a week. Which tray holds the seeds that have started to grow? Seeds need warmth and moisture to begin to grow, so the seeds in damp cotton in the warm spot should be the ones that have started to sprout.

Looking at Plant Growth

A plant's life cycle

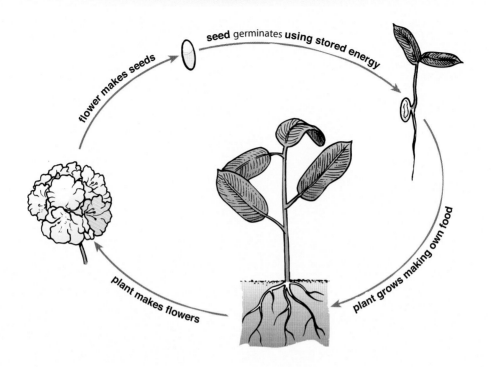

flower makes seeds

seed germinates **using stored energy**

plant grows making own food

plant makes flowers

Plants and growth cycles

Different plants have different growth cycles. **Annual** plants grow from **seed**, then flower, then spread seeds of their own, and finally die, all in less than one year. **Biennial** plants take two years to complete their life cycle, flowering in the second year. **Perennial** plants, such as trees and shrubs, live for two or more years, and most flower every year. The following lists show some of the plants that fall into these different categories.

Annual plants

Sunflower (*Helianthus*), African daisy (*Arctotis*), blazing star (*Bartonia*), marigold (*Calendula*), Californian poppy (*Eschscholzia*), gazania (*Gazania*), heliotrope (*Heliotropium*), candytuft (*Iberis*), sweet pea (*Lathyrus*), statice (*Limonium*), flax (*Linum*), virginia stock (*Malcolmia*), livingstone daisy (*Mesembryanthemum*), poppy (*Papaver*), African marigold (*Tagetes*), black-eyed Susan (*Thunbergia*), nasturtium (*Tropaeolum*)

Biennial plants

Canterbury bell (*Campanula medium*), wallflower (*Cheiranthus*), foxglove (*Digitalis purpurea*), honesty (*Lunaria*), forget-me-not (*Myosotis*), pansy (*Viola*), Sweet Williams (*Dianthus barbatus*), wild carrots

Perennial plants

African lily (*Agapanthus*), Japanese anemone (*Anemone*), columbine (*Aquilegia*), marsh marigold (*Calthia*), clematis (*Clematis*), pampas grass (*Cortaderia*), purple coneflower (*Echinacea*), globe thistle (*Echinops*), spurge (*Euphorbia*), sea holly (*Eryngium*), avens (*Geum*), plantain lily (*Hosta*), iris (*Iris*), lupin (*Lupinus*), maple (*Acer*), oak (*Quercus*), birch (*Betula*), redwood (*Sequoia*)

Transpiration and photosynthesis

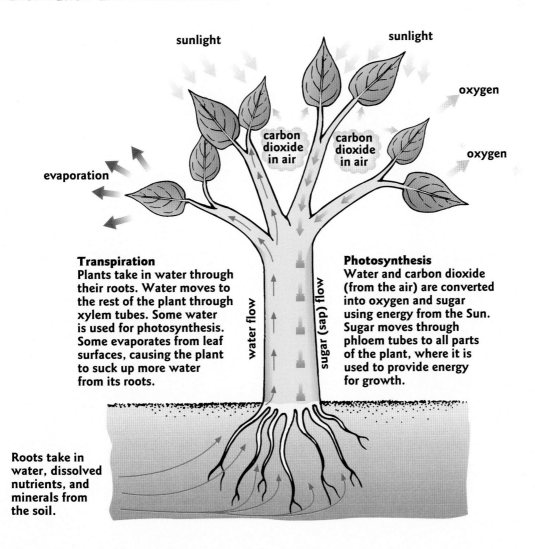

sunlight

sunlight

oxygen

carbon dioxide in air

carbon dioxide in air

oxygen

evaporation

Transpiration
Plants take in water through their roots. Water moves to the rest of the plant through xylem tubes. Some water is used for photosynthesis. Some evaporates from leaf surfaces, causing the plant to suck up more water from its roots.

water flow

sugar (sap) flow

Photosynthesis
Water and carbon dioxide (from the air) are converted into oxygen and sugar using energy from the Sun. Sugar moves through phloem tubes to all parts of the plant, where it is used to provide energy for growth.

Roots take in water, dissolved nutrients, and minerals from the soil.

Glossary

annual plant that grows, flowers, makes seeds, and dies all within one year (or season)

annual ring ring you can see when the trunk of a tree is cut down. If you count annual rings, you can find out how old a tree is.

bacteria microscopic organisms that are found in the soil, water, and air in all parts of Earth. Bacteria are the oldest and simplest living things. Some bacteria can bring about decay in dead plants and animals.

biennial plant that lives for two years. It usually flowers, makes seeds, and dies in the second year.

cambium layer of cells that are found between the xylem and phloem vessels in a plant

canopy uppermost layer of leafy branches in a forest

carbon dioxide gas in the air around us that plants use for photosynthesis

cell building block of living things that is so small it can only be seen with a microscope. Some microbes consist of a single cell, but most plants and animals are made up of millions or billions of cells.

chlorophyll green pigment found in plants that is used in photosynthesis. Chlorophyll gives leaves their green color.

chloroplast tiny compartment within plant cells. Photosynthesis happens in a plant's chloroplasts.

cork woody brown layer of dead cells found below the bark of a tree

cuticle waterproof layer covering the outside of a leaf

deciduous type of tree that loses all its leaves in winter. In cool climates, deciduous trees lose all their leaves before winter. In tropical areas, deciduous trees lose all their leaves at the start of the dry season.

decompose rot away by breaking down into smaller and smaller pieces

dissolve when something solid becomes a liquid

embryo very young plant that is contained in a seed

energy energy allows living things to do everything they need to live and grow. Plants and animals make the energy they need from their food.

evaporate when water turns from liquid into a vapor (an invisible gas). When clothes dry on a line, it is because the water evaporates and the vapor becomes part of the air.

fertilizer nutrient-rich powder or spray that plant-growers use to increase the amount or quality of their crop

fungi (singular is **fungus**) plant-like living things that do not make their food by photosynthesis and reproduce using spores. Mushrooms and toadstools are types of fungi.

germinate/germination when a seed starts to grow

gravity force that pulls things toward Earth and that stops us from floating off into space

grazing animal animal, such as a rabbit or deer, that eats living plants such as grass

habitat place in the natural world where a particular organism lives

hormone special chemical that makes plants grow

hormone rooting powder powder that has special chemicals in it, called hormones, that make plant parts grow. The powder can be added to a plant cutting to make a root grow.

irrigation watering of land by farmers, using pumps, sprays, or systems of canals and ditches, so that they can grow crops

meristem area on a plant where growth takes place. The meristems are often at the very tip of a shoot or root.

micrograph photograph taken through a microscope to show a clear, magnified image

mineral chemical building block of rocks. Plants need some minerals in order to grow and reproduce.

moss small green plant that grows in groups forming clumps and cushions close to the ground or rock on which they grow. Moss plants thrive in damp, shady habitats.

nectar sugary substance that plants make to attract insects, which like to eat it

nutrient chemical that plants and animals need in order to live

organism living thing, such as bacteria, cells, plants, and animals

oxygen gas in the air. Plants release oxygen into the air during the process of photosynthesis.

parasite plant (or animal) that lives on and steals food from another living thing

peat bog area of marshy ground formed from the partly rotted remains of a plant called bog moss. Peat has proven to be an excellent preservative. Things trapped inside peat can last a very long time without rotting away.

perennial plant that lives for more than two years, often for many years

phloem tubes that carry food (sugars) made in the leaf to all the other parts of the plant

photosynthesis process by which plants make their own food using water, carbon dioxide (a gas in the air), and energy from sunlight

pigment natural substance that gives color. Leaves are green because they contain a green pigment called chlorophyll.

respiration process by which living things release energy from their food

root plant part that grows underground and takes in water and nutrients

sap sugary liquid containing food made in the leaves. Sap flows in a plant's phloem tubes.

seed part of a plant that contains the beginnings of a new plant

shoot plant part that grows out and up from a seed and on which a plant's first leaves grow

species type of living thing

stalk part of the plant that attaches the leaf to the stem. Flower stalks attach little flowers to a stem.

stem part of a plant that holds the plant upright and supports its leaves and flowers

stomata (singular is **stoma**) tiny openings on a leaf, usually on the underside, that let water vapor and oxygen out and carbon dioxide in

tendril very long, thin leaf that wraps around supports to hold up a climbing plant

transpiration process by which water vapor is lost through the leaves of a plant

tropism growth response of plants or plant parts to outside factors, such as the availability of light, that are stronger from one direction than another

vascular plant plant that has xylem and phloem tubes for transporting water, nutrients, and food to its various parts

water vapor moisture that is suspended as droplets in air, having changed from a liquid state into a gas, like steam from a kettle

waxy waterproof substance that is a bit like plastic. Plants often have a very thin layer of natural wax around their leaves or fruit to stop these parts from drying out.

xylem tubes in a plant that carry water and nutrients from the roots to all the other parts of the plant

Further Information

Books

Burnie, David. *The Concise Nature Encyclopedia*. Boston: Kingfisher, 2006.

Burnie, David. *Eyewitness Guide: Tree*. New York: Dorling Kindersley, 2005.

Casper, Julie Kerr. *Natural Resources: Plants*. New York: Chelsea House, 2007.

Hipp, Andrew. *The Green World: Plant Diversity*. New York: Chelsea House, 2007.

Parker, Edward. *Rainforests: Trees and Plants*. Chicago: Raintree, 2003.

Riley, Peter. *Everyday Science: Plants*. Milwaukee: Gareth Stevens, 2004.

Silverstein, Alvin, Virginia Silverstein, and Laura Silverstein Nunn. *Science Concepts Second: Photosynthesis*. Brookfield, Conn.: Twenty-First Century Books, 2007.

Websites

www.mbgnet.net
At Missouri Botanical Garden's website, you can compare the habitats of the world.

www.kew.org/plants/titan/index.html
See the opening of the titan arum bud as well as lots of interesting information about one of the world's smelliest flowers.

www.urbanext.uiuc.edu/gpe/gpe.html
"The Great Plant Escape" is a fun way of learning about what different plant parts do. There is also a simple glossary of terms.

Conservation sites

These sites provide information on the dangers to wild plants and habitats and what conservation groups are doing to help them survive.

www.panda.org
The Worldwide Wildlife Fund works to protect animals and habitats.

www.sierraclub.org
The Sierra Club website provides information about the preservation work carried out by the group.

Places to visit

Many museums, arboretums (botanical gardens devoted to trees), and botanic gardens are fascinating places to visit. You could try:

United States Botanic Garden
245 First Street, S.W.
Washington, DC 20024
www.usbg.gov

New York Botanical Garden
Bronx River Parkway at Fordham Road
Bronx, NY 10458
www.nybg.org

Chicago Botanic Garden
1000 Lake Cook Road
Glencoe, IL 60022
www.chicagobotanic.org

Los Angeles County Arboretum & Botanic Garden
301 North Baldwin Avenue
Arcadia, CA 91007
www.arboretum.org

The State Botanical Garden of Georgia
2450 South Milledge Avenue
Athens, Georgia 30605
www.uga.edu/botgarden

You can also find out about plants by visiting local garden centers. The Latin names of plants will be on the plants' labels, so you can try to find as many related plants as you can.

Index